eXplore

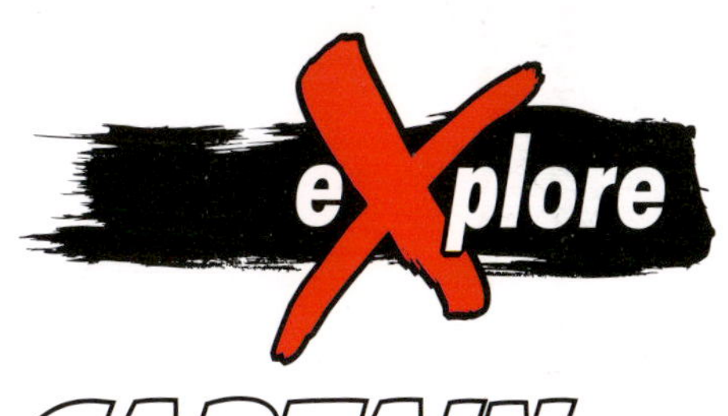

CAPTAIN JAMES COOK

The Pacific Explorer

R.T. Watts

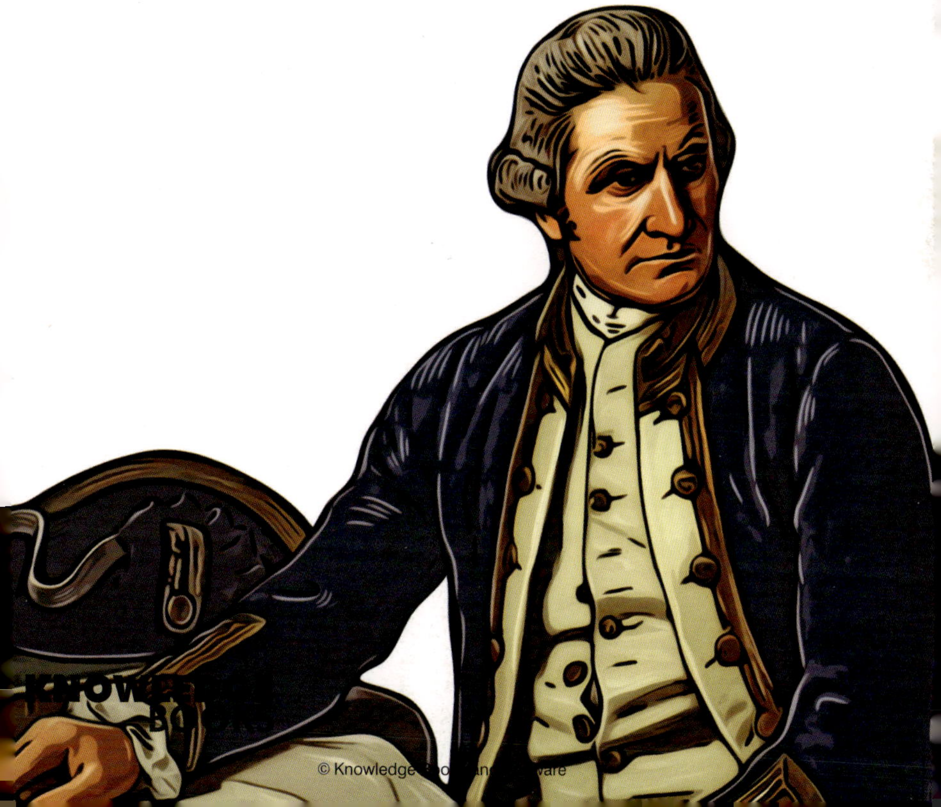

Teacher Notes:

James Cook was one of the greatest Pacific Ocean explorers and remains an inspirational character for students today. He was an outstanding sailor, navigator, and captain. Sentences, sight words, and complex words have been repetitively presented to make it easy to practice these words with increasing fluency throughout the story.

Discussion points for consideration:

1. The Transit of Venus was the reason given for the first voyage. Why did the British keep the exploration for the Great South Land a secret?

2. The health of the crew was essential to continue exploring. How did Cook manage this?

3. The Endeavour was correctly named for the first voyage. Why?

4. Why was Cook so successful in his voyages? Discuss teamwork, leadership, persistence, determination and resilience.

5. Cook set goals and achieved them, often in the face of hardship. Discuss some of your own goals and how you can go about achieving them.

Words to be introduced as sight words, difficult to decode words, and infrequent words before reading this book: Endeavour, commander, Canada, France, Britain, Adventure, Resolution, Discovery, Fitzroy, Melbourne, sauerkraut, Hawaii, Siberia, Continent, Antarctica, Batavia, Jakarta, panicked, navigator, exploration.

Contents

"Do what others say you can't do, and you will never pay attention to their limitations again."
Captain James Cook.

1. About James Cook

James Cook was born in November, 1728. He was a self-made sea captain. His father was a farm worker. James only went to school for five years. He was very good at maths. This got him a job as a shop boy. Later, he moved close to the port. He still worked as a shop boy but helped load the ships.

Cook's next job was in the stores on a ship. He sailed back and forth to America. Cook was slowly moving towards his goal of becoming a ship's captain. Cook was not wealthy or connected to famous people. He could only reach his goal by being better at his job.

This was the start of his sailing life. He moved from work in the food and equipment stores to help sail the ships.

He liked the sea and went into the navy. The navy had many jobs and provided lots of adventure. He was good at sailing ships and mapping. Cook mapped parts of Canada.

France and Britain were at war. The war was over which country would have control of Canada's colonies. Cook showed he was a brave and smart sailor. Cook helped catch many French boats. The navy knew he was a smart captain.

Cook did a lot of mapping, so he was the perfect person to explore the Pacific. The navy needed an explorer who was also good at map making. The captain needed to be a good sailor. A long trip needed a tough captain who could make sure everyone followed the rules. Cook was perfect for this job.

Maps could be used to explore the land. It allowed ships to travel and find their way to ports and towns.

A GENERAL CHART
OF THE ISLAND OF
NEWFOUNDLAND
with the Rocks & Soundings.
Drawn from SURVEYS taken by
ORDER of the RIGHT HONOURABLE the
LORDS COMMISSIONERS of the ADMIRALTY.
By
James Cook and Michael Lane Surveyors
and Others
LONDON
LABRADOR
BELL ISLE
ATLANTIC OCEAN
GULF OF S.T LAURENCE
NEWFOUNDLAND
BAY OF NOTRE DAME
CAPE S.T JOHN
CAPE FREELS
BONAVISTA
TRINITY BAY
CONCEPTION BAY
BAY OF PLACENTIA
S.T GEORGE'S BAY
CAPE ANGUILLE
CAPE RAY
FORTUNE BAY
BRETON I.

2. The Great South Land

Britain had plans to search for the Great South Land. This needed a captain who could also map the sea and the land. The navy finally gave Cook the job of being the captain of the ship.

The plans to explore for the Great South Land had to be kept secret. The French were also looking for this land. The British navy said they were going to Tahiti to watch the planet Venus transit in front of the Sun. The British were worried that the French would rush to get there first.

Explorers had been in the Pacific before Cook. The French had been to Tahiti. Dutch explorers had found New Holland (Australia) long before Cook.

Sailors had explored the northern, southern, and western parts of Australia, but not the eastern coast. Explorers had been to New Zealand. Abel Tasman, the Dutch explorer, had sailed around Tasmania. Cook was the first to explore the east coast of Australia.

3. The *Endeavour*

The *Endeavour* is now a very famous ship. "Endeavour" means to try hard to achieve a goal. This was a very well-chosen name for Cook's ship. One of NASA's Space Shuttles was also named the *Endeavour.* The *Endeavour* was refitted to be better for exploration. It was about 127 feet long. It was small and had 86 people on board. This included scientists such as Joseph Banks who looked at plants and animals.

The ship had to take food, water, goats for milk, and weapons for a long trip. Cook was going to stop along the way to get food and water. The time between stops was very long.

4. Scurvy

Today, if you feel sick we go and see a doctor. If you became ill on a sailing ship in those days, you were lucky to stay alive! Scurvy was a horrible sickness, and very painful. In Cook's time, over 2 million sailors had died from scurvy. It cut short many long trips because sailors died. Explorers on land got scurvy too! Cook was going on a very long sea voyage.

Long journeys without fresh food were the problem. Empty ships were seen on the sea filled with dead sailors. These ships floated across the seas for many years. They were called ghost ships! This image shows what scurvy looked like. It started with a rash on the body.

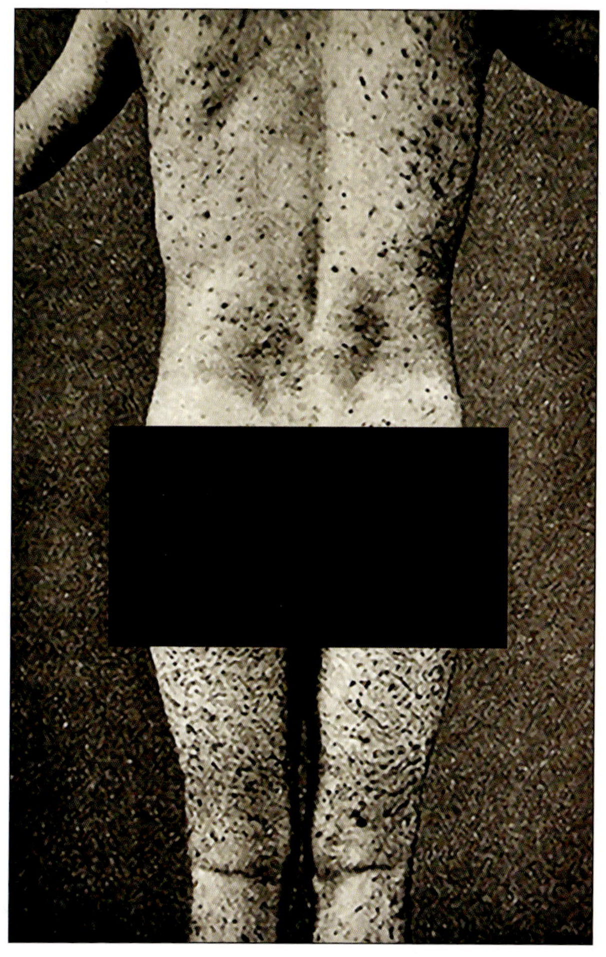

What is scurvy? Sailors got scurvy after a few months at sea. It starts with sore gums and spots. You feel very tired, like you have the flu. Your muscles, bones, and joints would ache. You get so tired, you stay in bed.

The skin shows more sores. Then the skin spots break, and blood starts coming out of the ulcers.

Your teeth begin to fall out, and you cannot eat as your mouth is too sore. You get very weak, and you sleep day and night. Soon after this, the pain only ends when you die.

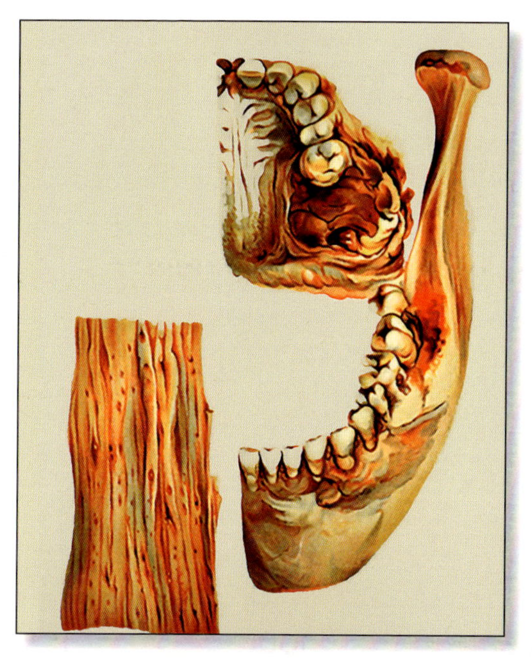

Cook was told about new ways to stop scurvy. He was told to take sauerkraut and lime juice. Sauerkraut is cabbage which is kept in a barrel. It is fermented, which means it is changed by bacteria. These good bacteria eat the cabbage juice to make a weak acid.

The sauerkraut's weak acid stops flies, bugs, fungus, and kills other critters. The sauerkraut can be eaten for many years. And it has ten times more Vitamin C than an orange!

The sailors did not want to eat the sauerkraut. Cook tricked them by pretending it was a treat for himself, Banks and the marines. Soon, everybody was eating sauerkraut.

One day on the trip, Cook saw his gums becoming red and sore. He saw spots on his face. Cook knew it was the start of scurvy, and was fast to take lime juice. Cook wrote that he was better in a week or two. His face lost the spots, and his gums were a healthy colour again. He had beaten scurvy by using lime juice and sauerkraut.

So what was special about lime juice and sauerkraut?

Scurvy is stopped by eating foods which have Vitamin C. This is a vitamin our bodies cannot make. We need to have it in our diets. Eating fresh fruits and vegetables is the easiest way to get Vitamin C. Very ill sailors with scurvy got better by eating foods containing Vitamin C.

5. The First Voyage

Cook made three voyages to the Pacific. The first voyage left England in August,1768 and sailed south towards Africa. He first stopped in September at Madeira, in the Canary Islands. Here, he got fresh food and water.

On the next part, he followed the coast of Africa. He then sailed down towards South America and stopped for supplies in November, 1768. As he sailed south, it got freezing cold and windy. He was aiming for Cape Horn at the bottom of South America.

Cook stopped again for water and firewood in January, 1769. He had sailed over 8,000 miles in 5 months or about 62 miles per day.

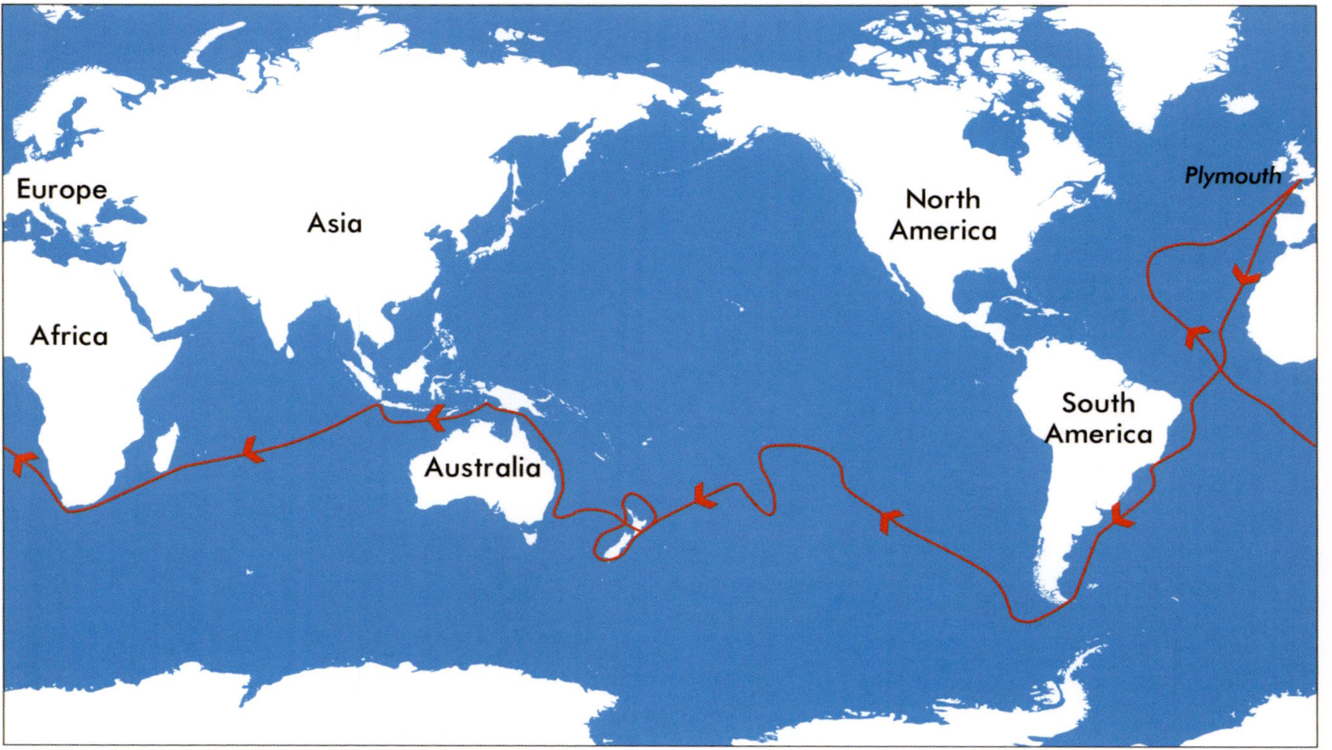

Europe
Asia
North America
Plymouth
Africa
Australia
South America

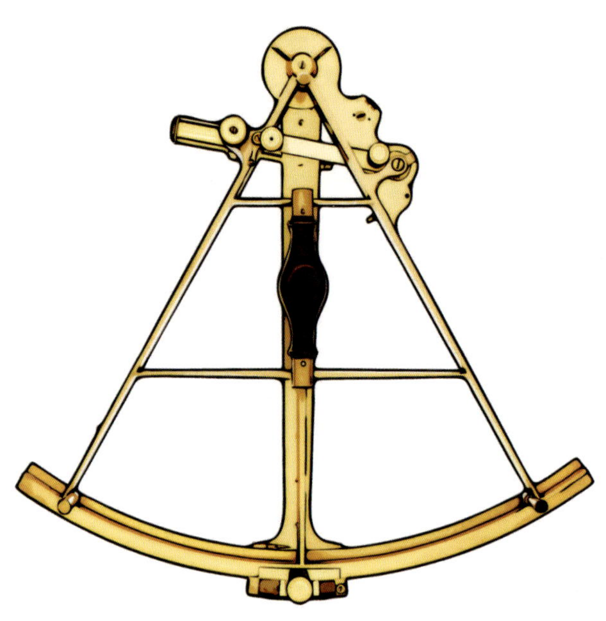

Cook was now in the Pacific Ocean, and he sailed north towards Tahiti. He finally arrived in Tahiti in April, 1770. The plan was to study the planet Venus as it went in front of the Sun in June that year. By studying this they hoped to work out the distance to the Sun.

The next stage was to look for the Great South Land. Cook left Tahiti and sailed south looking for the Great South Land. The *Endeavour* sailed for 3 months searching. Cook then turned west and sailed for New Zealand, which he already knew was there. He mapped all of New Zealand for 6 months.

In March, 1770 Cook headed west towards Australia. He knew that there was land there because the Dutch explorers had made charts of the west and south of Australia. Maps were not made of the east coast of Australia.

Cook arrived off the coast of Australia in April, 1770. He sailed north and landed in Botany Bay. He then charted the east coast of Australia.

Asia
Australia

6. Coral Reef Damage

Cook continued sailing north to the top of Australia. He was close to the end of the reef when he struck coral. The crew did not see the reef because it was just below the water. Sailors today call it a 'bombie'. The ship was stuck on the coral reef. The ship was taking on water, and was going to sink. If it sank, the whole crew would have been trapped about 30 miles from the shore. It was a terrifying time for them all.

They used sails to patch the outside of the boat to stop the leak. They kept pumping the water out of the ship. Cook removed over 50 tons of goods from the ship. He took off the cannons, barrels, and stone ballast which was used to steady the boat.

Cook was smart enough to re-float the ship at high tide. He moved the ship off the reef and sailed it towards the coast. They landed on a sandy beach beside a river. The crew repaired the hole with new wood in 6 weeks, and the ship was ready to sail again. This location is now known as Cooktown.

Cook's plan to sail back across the Pacific to England had to be changed. The *Endeavour* was now too weak to sail through the bad storms around South America. The boat had a repaired hole which needed to be fixed properly. The ship also had marine worms which had eaten into the wood. This made the ship very weak.

7. Batavia

The next part of the journey was to go up to Java. The place was called Batavia and is now called Jakarta.

At this stage, Captain Cook had kept the crew alive. The crew were in good health after being away for over 18 months. No captain had done this!

However, when they reached Batavia, there was an outbreak of typhoid fever. Typhoid fever is caused by unclean water, and it causes your digestive system to lose all its fluid. You cannot stop going to the toilet.

Captain Cook lost over 30 of his crew in Batavia. They died from typhoid fever and malaria.

Europe
Asia
Africa
Australia

Cook left Batavia (Jakarta) for the Cape of Good Hope in South Africa. He then travelled along the African coast to England. After three years of sailing in the Pacific and around the world, Cook arrived back in England in July, 1771.

After the voyage, Cook was made a commander which was a great honour. Cook had looked for the Great South Land and mapped New Zealand. He had mapped the east coast of Australia. Australia was of great interest as Britain saw a chance to expand its empire and make wealth.

8. Second Voyage

The next voyage was to look again for the Great South Land. There were two ships, the *Resolution* and the *Adventure.* Cook commanded the *Resolution.*

Cook had charted New Zealand and the east coast of Australia. But the British believed there was a land south of Australia and they wanted to find it.

This was an amazing voyage, as it took Cook right into the ice of Antarctica. After reaching Tahiti again they sailed south looking for the Great South Land.

This time they really did go as far south as possible. The sails of the boat were covered in ice.

urope
Asia
Africa
Australia

They went south of Macquarie and
Heard Islands. This meant they got
close to the land of Antarctica.

The ships lost sight of each other, and
the *HMS Adventure* turned back
towards New Zealand.

Cook continued to search. He
returned to Tahiti and then sailed
south again to search for the Great
South Land. He realised there was
only the giant ice continent. He was
very close to Antarctica.

He then turned for home. They
stopped at islands off South America
in the Atlantic before heading back to
England.

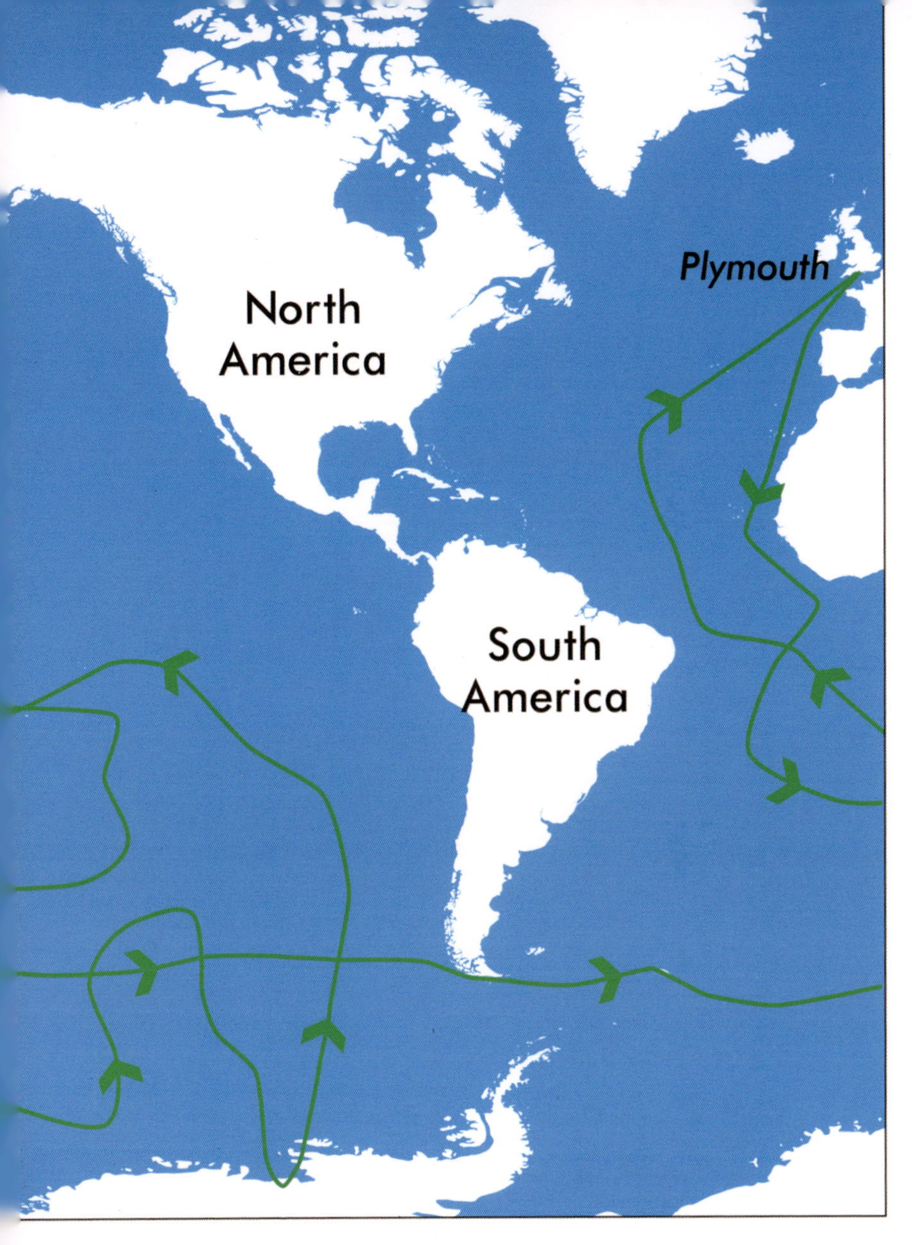

Plymouth
North America
South America

9. Third Voyage

Commander James Cook's third mission was in the north Pacific. There were two ships: *Resolution* again, and *Discovery*. The mission was to explore the north Pacific for a sea passage around Canada into the top of the Atlantic near Europe. This search made good sense as it would be a fast way back to England from Asia and the Pacific. This passage was called the Northwest Passage and it is still being explored today.

Cook never found the Northwest Passage as it was frozen through the summer as well as winter.

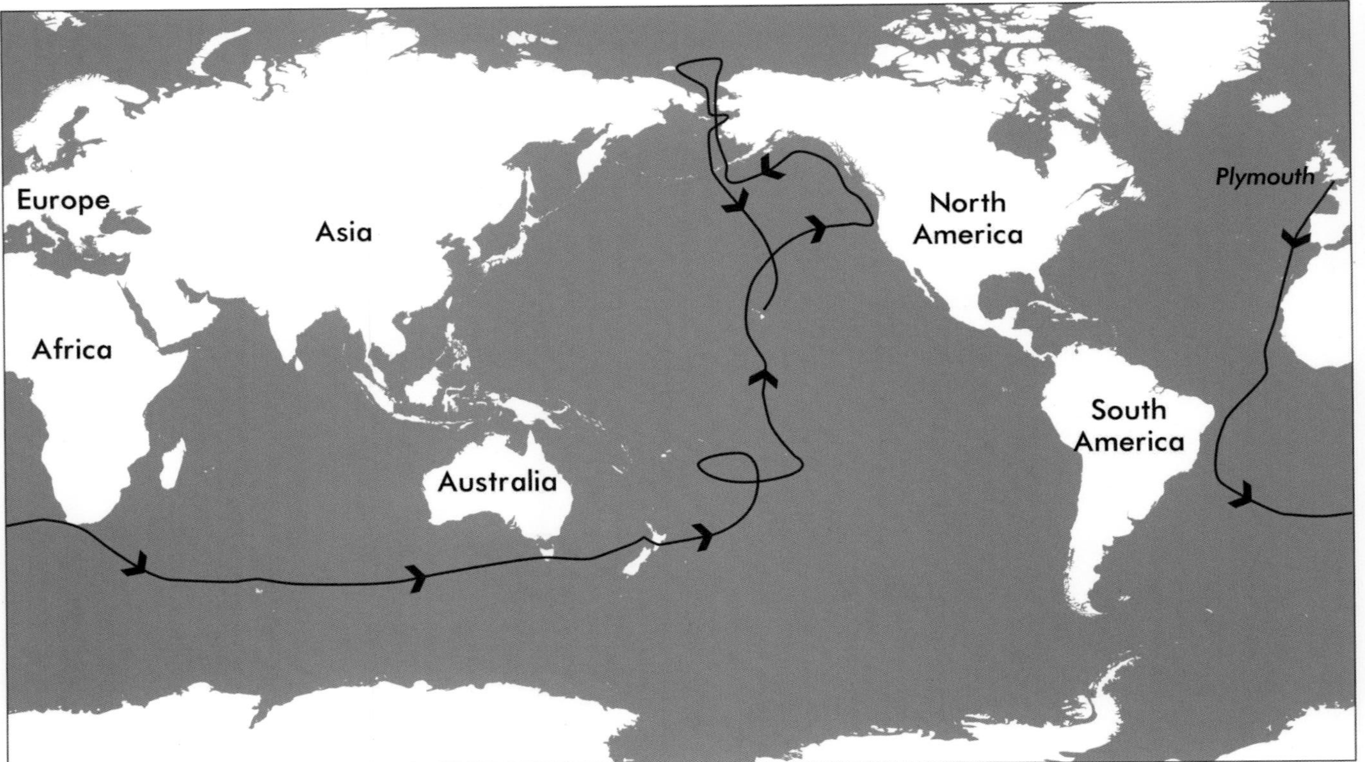

Europe
Asia
Africa
North America
Australia
South America
Plymouth

After Tahiti, Cook sailed north and explored Hawaii. Cook called these the Sandwich Islands after Lord Sandwich.

He sailed north and mapped along America all the way to Alaska. He then mapped the top part of Siberia. He was looking for the Northwest Passage which would take him across the top of Canada. Cook was stopped by frozen seas.

Cook sailed south again to Hawaii and mapped the islands. He was getting on well with the Hawaiian people when disputes started over a stolen boat that Cook wanted back. He decided to take the chief as a hostage but this was a bad move. The local people panicked and started attacking him.

He was clubbed and stabbed by the Hawaiian people. He died on the beach.

Cook was an incredible person. He was a great sailor and navigator. He went to so many dangerous places and he seemed fearless. He was so precise in his measurements that his maps worked for hundreds of years.

He looked after his crew and made sure they were kept healthy. He explored most of the Pacific from top to bottom. He was not interested in sitting back enjoying the glory – he wanted to keep exploring!

Today, his simple cottage is now in Melbourne at the Fitzroy Gardens. It is a special place for the great explorer of the Pacific.

Word Bank

Endeavour

commander

Canada

France

Britain

Adventure

Resolution

Discovery

Fitzroy

Melbourne

sauerkraut

Hawaii

Siberia

continent

Antarctica

Batavia

Jakarta

panicked

equipment

voyage

Tahiti

New Zealand

exploration

scientists